THE SPIRES OF OXFORD
AND OTHER POEMS

BY
W. M. LETTS
AUTHOR OF "SONGS FROM LEINSTER," "A ROUGH WAY,"
"DIANA DETHRONED," ETC.

NEW YORK
E. P. DUTTON AND COMPANY
681 FIFTH AVENUE
1917

PUBLISHERS' NOTE

The majority of the Poems in this volume were published by us in 1916 under the title *Hallow-e'en and Poems of the War*.

The verdict of the public, as shown by continual requests for permission to republish, is that *The Spires of Oxford* is the most important poem in the volume —and therefore in issuing a new edition with several new poems, we bow to this verdict and give *The Spires of Oxford* its place in the forefront of the volume.

THE PUBLISHERS

Certain of these poems have already appeared in the *Spectator*, *Westminster Gazette*, *Pall Mall Gazette*, *Observer*, *Dublin Review*, and *The Month*.

*To you who see
The world with me
I give this book.*

*If you in courtesy should look
With favour on its pages claim
The title deed and write your name
Here on this page. To you who know
The glamour of the passing show,
Sublime and sordid trivial, great,
But life,—this book I dedicate.
As casual lookers-on we meet
Here at some corner of the street.
It's good to know you see it too,
Smile, sigh and wonder when I do;
That you discern the crooked jest
Of contrast 'twixt our worst and best,
Humour is ever friendship's test.
I like to know you hear the call
Of all things sad, neglected, small;
Thrill to the magic of the wind,
Love country, town and your own kind,
Sinners and saints and sea and sky
Just as they are, for so do I.*

*Then let this book
I fain would mend
Be yours, my friend.*

CONTENTS

POEMS OF THE WAR

	PAGE
THE SPIRES OF OXFORD	3
HALLOW-E'EN, 1915	5
HALLOW-E'EN, 1914	7
THE CALL TO ARMS IN OUR STREET	9
CHAPLAIN TO THE FORCES	11
CASUALTY	13
PRO PATRIA	15
GOLDEN BOYS	16
IN THE MAKING	17
EPIPHANY, 1916	19
SCREENS	21
WHAT REWARD?	23
TO A SOLDIER IN HOSPITAL	24
JULY, 1916	27
HE PRAYED	29
THE DESERTER	30
A SISTER IN A MILITARY HOSPITAL	32

AD MORTUUM

DEAD	35
YOUR NAME	36
HEART'S DESIRE	37
LOSS	38

CONTENTS

	PAGE
The Dream	39
In Memory	40
If Love of Mine	41
Alive	42
In All Loveliness	43
In Town	44
Spring the Cheat	45
The Magic City	46
The Ghost	47
The Truce	48

MISCELLANEA

Rosa Mystica	51
The Winds at Bethlehem	53
Offering	55
Sonia's Song	56
The Wish	58
Home	60
The Wind's Call	64
Elaine at Astolat	66
The Page's Song of the Happy Lady	67
Faëries	69
To Tim	71
A Dog's Grave	73
To Scott	74
The Monkey's Carol	75
Pensioners	77
Lookers-on	79
Friends	80
Angelic Service	82
Our Lady of the Lupins	84
The Doctor	86
Sails	101
The Rebel	103
Aeroplanes and Dragonflies	104
The Trust	105

THE SPIRES OF OXFORD

(SEEN FROM A TRAIN)

I saw the spires of Oxford
   As I was passing by,
The grey spires of Oxford
   Against a pearl-grey sky;
My heart was with the Oxford men
   Who went abroad to die.

The years go fast in Oxford,
   The golden years and gay;
The hoary colleges look down
   On careless boys at play,
But when the bugles sounded—War!
   They put their games away.

They left the peaceful river,
   The cricket field, the quad,
The shaven lawns of Oxford
   To seek a bloody sod.
They gave their merry youth away
   For country and for God.

THE SPIRES OF OXFORD

God rest you, happy gentlemen,
    Who laid your good lives down,
Who took the khaki and the gun
    Instead of cap and gown.
God bring you to a fairer place
    Than even Oxford town.

HALLOW-E'EN, 1915

WILL you come back to us, men of our hearts, to-night
In the misty close of the brief October day?
Will you leave the alien graves where you sleep and steal away
To see the gables and eaves of home grow dark in the evening light?

O men of the manor and moated hall and farm,
Come back to-night, treading softly over the grass;
The dew of the autumn dusk will not betray where you pass;
The watchful dog may stir in his sleep but he'll raise no hoarse alarm.

Then you will stand, not strangers, but wishful to look
At the kindly lamplight shed from the open door,

And the fire-lit casement where one, having wept
    you sore,
Sits dreaming alone with her sorrow, not heeding
    her open book.

Forgotten awhile the weary trenches, the dome
Of pitiless Eastern sky, in this quiet hour
When no sound breaks the hush but the chimes
    from the old church tower,
And the river's song at the weir,—ah! then we will
    welcome you home.

You will come back to us just as the robin sings
Nunc Dimittis from the larch to a sun late set
In purple woodlands; when caught like silver fish
    in a net
The stars gleam out through the orchard boughs
    and the church owl flaps his wings.

We have no fear of you, silent shadows, who tread
The leaf-bestrewn paths, the dew-wet lawns. Draw
    near
To the glowing fire, the empty chair,—we shall not
    fear,
Being but ghosts for the lack of you, ghosts of our
    well-beloved dead.

HALLOW-E'EN, 1914

"Why do you wait at your door, woman,
   Alone in the night?"
"I am waiting for one who will come, stranger,
   To show him a light.
He will see me afar on the road
   And be glad at the sight."

"Have you no fear in your heart, woman,
   To stand there alone?
There is comfort for you and kindly content
   Beside the hearthstone."
But she answered, "No rest can I have
   Till I welcome my own."

"Is it far he must travel to-night,
   This man of your heart?"
"Strange lands that I know not and pitiless seas
   Have kept us apart,
And he travels this night to his home
   Without guide, without chart."

"And has he companions to cheer him?"
  "Aye, many," she said.
"The candles are lighted, the hearthstones are
    swept,
  The fires glow red.
We shall welcome them out of the night—
  Our home-coming dead."

THE CALL TO ARMS IN OUR STREET

There's a woman sobs her heart out,
  With her head against the door,
For the man that's called to leave her,
  —God have pity on the poor!
    But it's beat, drums, beat,
      While the lads march down the street,
    And it's blow, trumpets, blow,
      Keep your tears until they go.

There's a crowd of little children
  Who march along and shout,
For it's fine to play at soldiers
  Now their fathers are called out.
    So it's beat, drums, beat;
      But who'll find them food to eat?
    And it's blow, trumpets, blow,
      Ah! the children little know.

THE CALL TO ARMS IN OUR STREET

There's a mother who stands watching
　For the last look of her son,
A worn poor widow woman
　And he her only one.
　　But it's beat, drums, beat,
　　Though God knows when we shall meet;
　　And it's blow, trumpets, blow:
　　We must smile and cheer them so.

There's a young girl who stands laughing,
　For she thinks a war is grand,
And it's fine to see the lads pass,
　And it's fine to hear the band.
　　So it's beat, drums, beat,
　　To the fall of many feet;
　　And it's blow, trumpets, blow,
　　God go with you where you go
　　To the war.

CHAPLAIN TO THE FORCES

Ambassador of Christ you go
   Up to the very gates of hell,
   Through fog of powder, storm of shell,
To speak your Master's message: "Lo,
   The Prince of Peace is with you still,
   His peace be with you, His goodwill."

It is not small, your priesthood's price,
   To be a man and yet stand by,
   To hold your life whilst others die,
To bless, not share the sacrifice,
   To watch the strife and take no part—
   You with the fire at your heart.

But yours, for our great Captain Christ
   To know the sweat of agony,
   The darkness of Gethsemane
In anguish for these souls unpriced.
   Vicegerent of God's pity you,
   'A sword must pierce your own soul through!

CHAPLAIN TO THE FORCES

In the pale gleam of new-born day
  Apart in some tree-shadowed place,
  Your altar but a packing case,
Rude as the shed where Mary lay,
  Your sanctuary the rain-drenched sod
  You bring the kneeling soldier, God.

As sentinel you guard the gate
  'Twixt life and death, and unto death
  Speed the brave soul whose failing breath
Shudders not at the grip of Fate,
  But answers, gallant to the end,
  "Christ is the Word—and I His friend."

Then God go with you, priest of God,
  For all is well and shall be well.
  What though you tread the roads of hell?
With nail-pierced feet these ways He trod.
  Above the anguish and the loss
  Still floats the ensign of His Cross.

CASUALTY

John Delaney of the Rifles has been shot.
  A man we never knew,
  Does it cloud the day for you
  That he lies among the dead
Moving, hearing, heeding not?

No history will hold his humble name.
  No sculptured stone will tell
  The traveller where he fell;
  That he lies among the dead
Is the measure of his fame.

When our troops return victorious shall we c(
  That deaf to all the cheers,
  Lacking tribute of our tears,
  He is lying with the dead
Stark and silent, God knows where?

CASUALTY

John Delaney of the Rifles—who was he?
  A name seen on a list
  All unknown and all unmissed.
  What to us that he is dead?—
Yet he died for you and me.

PRO PATRIA

In bowler hats, top coats,
With woollen mufflers round their throats,
    They played at war,
These men I watched to-day.
Weary with office work, pinched-faced, depressed,
About the field they marched and counter-marched,
Halting and marking time and all the rest—
Meanwhile the world went on its way
To see the football heroes play.

No music, no applause,
No splendour for them but a Cause
    Hid deep at heart.
They drilled there soberly,
Their one half-holiday—the various show
Of theatres all resisted, home renounced;
The Picture Palace with its kindly glow
Forgotten now, that they may be
Worthy of England's chivalry.

GOLDEN BOYS

Not harps and palms for these, O God,
Nor endless rest within the courts of Heaven,—
These happy boys who left the football field,
The hockey ground, the river, the eleven,
In a far grimmer game, with high elated souls
To score their goals.

Let these, O God, still test their manhood's
    strength,
Wrestle and leap and run,
Feel sea and wind and sun;
With Cherubim contend;
The timeless morning spend
In great celestial games.
Let there be laughter and a merry noise
Now that the fields of Heaven shine
With all these golden boys.

IN THE MAKING

"And of all knights—I out-take none, say what men will say—he beareth the flower of all chivalry."—MALORY.

God took fine clay and made a man
    As brave and true, as clean and straight
As any since the world began,
    And men were first at odds with fate.

His was the knighthood of a soul
    Whose faith and honour cannot fail.
The Far-off City was his goal,
    His quest the vision of Sancgreal.

Born of the race that sailed the sea
    With Hawke and Frobisher and Drake,
He too could face death merrily
    And risk his all and never quake.

Fearless and gentle, steel and fire,
    Son of an order passing hence.
He rode like any old-time squire,
    Rode straight and never shirked a fence.

IN THE MAKING

What did he lack, what one thing more?
   They could not tell who loved him best.
Only they saw God try him sore
   And put his valour to the test.

From death upon the battlefield
   He had not shrunk nor turned away.
But stauncher still he would not yield
   To the long siege of every day.

He would not wince nor show the pain
   Of that slow ordeal by fire.
He set his face and laughed again
   Before his shattered heart's desire.

So God approved the deep-laid plan
   We, blind-eyed, had not understood.
God said "Behold, a gentleman,"
   And smiled and saw His work was good.

EPIPHANY, 1916

The Kings still come to Bethlehem
   Though nineteen centuries have fled;
The Kings still come to Bethlehem
   To worship at a Baby's bed.
And still a star shines in the East,
For sage and soldier, king and priest.

They come not as they came of old
   On lordly camels richly dight;
They come not bearing myrrh and gold
   And jewels for a king's delight.
All battle-stained and grim are they
Who seek the Prince of Peace to-day.

They bring not pearls nor frankincense
   To offer Him for His content.
Weary and worn with long suspense
   With kingdoms ravished, fortunes spent,
They have no gifts to bring but these—
Men's blood and women's agonies.

EPIPHANY, 1916

What toys have they to please a child?
    Cannon and gun and bayonet.
What gold?   Their honour undefiled.
    What myrrh?   Sad hearts and long regret.
For they have found through bitter loss
That Kings are throned upon the cross.

The Kings still come to Bethlehem
    With broken hearts and souls sore-vexed.
And still the star is guiding them
    Through weary nights and days perplexed.
God greet you, Kings, that you may be
New-crowned at His Epiphany.

SCREENS

(IN A HOSPITAL)

They put the screens around his bed;
   A crumpled heap I saw him lie,
White counterpane and rough dark head,
   Those screens—they showed that he would die

They put the screens about his bed;
   We might not play the gramophone,
And so we played at cards instead
   And left him dying there alone.

The covers on the screen are red,
   The counterpanes are white and clean;—
He might have lived and loved and wed
   But now he's done for at nineteen.

An ounce or more of Turkish lead,
   He got his wounds at Suvla Bay;
They've brought the Union Jack to spread
   Upon him when he goes away.

SCREENS

He'll want those three red screens no more,
   Another man will get his bed,
We'll make the row we did before
   But—Jove!—I'm sorry that he's dead.

WHAT REWARD?

You gave your life, boy,
   And *you* gave a limb:
But he who gave his precious wits,
   Say, what reward for him?

One has his glory,
   One has found his rest.
But what of this poor babbler here
   With chin sunk on his breast?

Flotsam of battle,
   With brain bemused and dim,
O God, for such a sacrifice
   Say, what reward for him?

TO A SOLDIER IN HOSPITAL

(A. W.)

COURAGE came to you with your boyhood's grace
    Of ardent life and limb.
Each day new dangers steeled you to the test,
    To ride, to climb, to swim.
Your hot blood taught you carelessness of death
With every breath.

So when you went to play another game
    You could not but be brave:
An Empire's team, a rougher football field,
    The end—who knew?—your grave.
What matter? On the winning of a goal
You staked your soul.

Yes, you wore courage as you wore your youth,
    With carelessness and joy.
But in what Spartan school of discipline
    Did you get patience, boy?
How did you learn to bear this long-drawn pain
And not complain?

TO A SOLDIER IN HOSPITAL

Restless with throbbing hopes, with thwarted aims,
    Impulsive as a colt,
How do you lie here month by weary month,
    Helpless and not revolt?
What joy can these monotonous days afford
Here in a ward?

Yet you are merry as the spring-time birds
    Or feign the gaiety
Lest those who dress and tend your wound each
    day.
    Should guess the agony,
Lest they should suffer—this the only fear
You let draw near.

Greybeard philosophy has sought in books
    And argument this truth,—
That man is greater than his pain, but you
    Have learnt it in your youth.
You know the wisdom taught by Calvary
At twenty-three.

Death would have found you brave, but braver
    still
    You face each weary day,

TO A SOLDIER IN HOSPITAL

A merry Stoic, patient, chivalrous,
    Divinely kind and gay.
You bear your knowledge lightly, graduate
Of unkind Fate.

Careless philosopher, the first to laugh,
    The latest to complain;
Unmindful that you teach, you taught me this
    In your long fight with pain;
Since God made man so good,—here stands my
    creed,
—God's good indeed.

JULY, 1916

Here in happy England the fields are steeped in
  quiet,
  Saving for larks' song and drone of bumble bees;
The deep lanes are decked with roses all a-riot,
  With bryony and vetch and ferny tapestries.
O here a maid would linger to hear the blackbird
  fluting,
  And here a lad might pause by wind-berippled
  wheat,
The lovers in the bat's light would hear the brown
  owl hooting,
  Before the latticed lights of home recalled their
  lagging feet.

. . . . . .

But over there, in France, the grass is torn and
  trodden,
  Our pastures grow moon daisies, but *theirs* are
  strewn with lead.
The fertile, kindly fields are harassed and blood-
  sodden,
  The sheaves they bear for harvesting will be our
  garnered dead.

But there the lads of England, in peril of advancing,
    Have laid their splendid lives down, ungrudging of the cost;
The record—just their names here—means a moment's careless glancing,
    But who can tell the promise, the fulfilment of our lost?

    .   .   .   .   .   .

Here in happy England the Summer pours her treasure
    Of grasses, of flowers before our heedless feet.
The swallow-haunted streams meander at their pleasure
    Through loosestrife and rushes and plumèd meadow-sweet.
Yet how shall we forget them, the young men, the splendid,
    Who left this golden heritage, who put the Summer by,
Who kept for us our England inviolate, defended,
    But by their passing made for us December of July?

HE PRAYED

He prayed,
There where he lay,
Blood-sodden and unkempt,
As never in his young carelessness he'd dreamt
That he could pray.

He prayed;
Not that the pain should cease,
Nor yet for water in the parching heat,
Nor for death's quick release,
Nor even for the tardy feet
Of stretcher-bearers bringing aid.

He prayed;
Cast helpless on the bloody sod:
"Don't trouble now, O God, for me,
But keep the boys. Go forward with them, God!
O speed the Camerons to victory."
The kilts flashed on: "Well played," he sighed,
   "well played."
Just so he prayed.

THE DESERTER

There was a man,—don't mind his name,
Whom Fear had dogged by night and day.
He could not face the German guns
And so he turned and ran away.
Just that—he turned and ran away,
But who can judge him, you or I?
God makes a man of flesh and blood
Who yearns to live and not to die.
And this man when he feared to die
Was scared as any frightened child,
His knees were shaking under him,
His breath came fast, his eyes were wild.
I've seen a hare with eyes as wild,
With throbbing heart and sobbing breath.
But oh! it shames one's soul to see
A man in abject fear of death.
But fear had gripped him, so had death;
His number had gone up that day,
They might not heed his frightened eyes,
They shot him when the dawn was grey.

THE DESERTER

Blindfolded, when the dawn was grey,
He stood there in a place apart,
The shots rang out and down he fell,
An English bullet in his heart.
An English bullet in his heart!
But here's the irony of life,—
His mother thinks he fought and fell
A hero, foremost in the strife.
So she goes proudly; to the strife
Her best, her hero son she gave.
O well for her she does not know
He lies in a deserter's grave.

A SISTER IN A MILITARY HOSPITAL

Blue dress, blue tippet, trimmed with red,
White veil, coif-like about her head.
Starched apron, cuffs, and cool, kind hands,
Trained servants to her quick commands.
Swift feet that lag not to obey
In diligent service day by day.

A face that would have brought delight
To some pure-souled pre-Raphaelite;
Madonna of a moment, caught
Unwary in the toils of thought,
Stilled in her tireless energy,
Dark-eyed and hushed with sympathy.

Warm, eager as the south-west wind,
Straight as a larch and gaily kind
As pinewood fires on winter eves,
Wholesome and young as April leaves,
Four seasons blent in rare accord
—You have the Sister of our ward.

*For England's sake men give their lives
And we cry "Brave."
But braver yet
The hearts that break and live
Having no more to give,
Mothers, sweethearts and wives.
Let none forget
Or with averted head
Pass this great sorrow by—
These would how thankfully be dead
Yet may not die.*

DEAD

In misty cerements they wrapped the word
My heart had feared so long: dead ... dead ...
    I heard
But marvelled they could think the thing was true
Because death cannot be for such as you.
So while they spoke kind words to suit my need
Of foolish idle things my heart took heed,
Your racquet and a worn-out tennis shoe,
Your pipe upon the mantel,—then a bird
Upon the wind-tossed larch began to sing
And I remembered how one day in Spring
You found the wren's nest in the wall and said
"Hush! ... listen! I can hear them quarrel-
    ling ..."
The tennis court is marked, the wrens are fled,
But you are dead, belovèd, you are dead.

YOUR NAME

When I can dare at last to speak your name
It shall not be with hushed and reverent speech
As if your spirit were beyond the reach
Of homely merry things, kind jest or game.
Death shall not hide you in some jewelled shrine
Nor set you in marmoreal pomp apart,
You who still share the ingle of my heart,
Participant in every thought of mine.

Your name, when I can dare to speak it, dear,
Shall still be linked with laughter and with joy.
No solemn panegyrist shall destroy
My image of you, gay, familiar
As in old happy days,—lest I discover
Too late I've won a saint but lost a lover.

HEART'S DESIRE

My heart's desire was like a garden seen
On sudden through the opening of a door
In the grey street of life, unguessed before
But now how magic in sun-smitten green:
Wide cedar-shaded lawns, the glow and sheen
Of borders decked with all a gardener's lore,
Long shaven hedges of old yew, hung o'er
With gossamer, wide paths to please a queen,
Whose happy silken skirts would brush the dew
From peonies and lupins white and blue.
Enchanted, there I lingered for a space,
Forgetful of the street, of tasks to do.
But when I would have entered that sweet place
The wind rose and the door slammed in my face.

LOSS

In losing you I lost my sun and moon
And all the stars that blessed my lonely night.
I lost the hope of Spring, the joy of June,
The Autumn's peace, the Winter's firelight.
I lost the zest of living, the sweet sense
Expectant of your step, your smile, your kiss;
I lost all hope and fear and keen suspense
For this cold calm, sans agony, sans bliss.
I lost the rainbow's gold, the silver key
That gave me freedom of my town of dreams;
I lost the path that leads to Faërie
By beechen glades and heron-haunted streams.
I lost the master word, dear love, the clue
That threads the maze of life when I lost you.

THE DREAM

I DREAMT—before death made such dreaming
    vain—
That sometime, on a day of wind and rain,
I would come home to you at fall of night
And see your window flushed with firelight.
There in the chill dark lonesomeness I'd wait
A moment, standing at the garden gate
Scarce trusting that my happiness was true,—
The kind warm lights of home and love and you.

Then, lest they'd vanish to be mine no more,
I'd speed my steps along the garden path,
Cross my own threshold, close the wind-blown door
And find you in the firelight of the hearth.
O happiness! to kneel beside you there
And feel your fingers resting on my hair.

IN MEMORY

Would God that I might build my love in stone
That would out-time the centuries and dare
Despiteful death to lay his finger there,
So that your fame to all men might be known;
A minster church, crowned with a soaring spire,
Great buttressed walls, clerestory, lofty nave
Deep carven doors and every window brave
With sunset hues. In chantry, transept, choir,
So great a peace men needs must kneel to pray.
Then I would have them, each to other say,
"One loved her true love well and worthily
And built this minster to his memory,
God rest their souls"—so all should know the story,
Your fame, belovèd, and God's greater glory.

IF LOVE OF MINE

If love of mine could witch you back to earth
It would be when the bat is on the wing,
The lawn dew-drenched, the first stars glimmering,
The moon a golden slip of seven nights' birth.
If prayer of mine could bring you it would be
To this wraith-flowered jasmine-scented place
Where shadow trees their branches interlace;
Phantoms we'd tread a land of fantasy.
If love could hold you I would bid you wait
Till the pearl sky is indigo and till
The plough show silver lamps beyond the hill
And Aldebaran burns above the gate.

If love of mine could lure you back to me
From the rose gardens of eternity.

ALIVE

Because you live, though out of sight and reach,
I will, so help me God, live bravely too,
Taking the road with laughter and gay speech,
Alert, intent to give life all its due.
I will delight my soul with many things,
The humours of the street and books and plays,
Great rocks and waves winnowed by seagulls'
    wings,
Star-jewelled Winter nights, gold harvest days.

I will for your sake praise what I have missed,
The sweet content of long-united lives,
The sunrise joy of lovers who have kissed,
Children with flower-faces, happy wives.
And last I will praise Death who gives anew
Brave life adventurous and love—and you.

IN ALL LOVELINESS

I LOVE you in all loveliness, sweetheart.
Skies, stars, and flowers speak of you to me
And every season is your emissary
Lest I forget you now we are apart.

The tracery of leafless trees inset
Upon a saffron sky: warm nights in June
When corncrakes shout beneath a full low moon;
September mornings in a world dew-wet;
Dim harvest fields at dusk: tree-shadowed lawns,
A garden sweet with lavender and stocks;
Pale flowers by twilight, jessamine and phlox;
The ring-doves' soft complaint in summer dawns;
The scent of cowslips, violets white and blue—
These are the embassies that speak of you!

IN TOWN

I love you in the vehement life of town,
The pulsing high-ways, the gay market places:
The masque of various players, king and clown,
Philosopher and fool: the passing faces;
The sense of brotherhood with all I meet.
I love you in the wonder of night's falling,
The blossoming of lights in every street,
The pearl-shell sky, pale river, voices calling
The news of town: the homeward-pressing throng,
The gay shop windows with their varied treasure;
Street melody, a snatch of careless song,
Lovers arm-linked, the carnival of pleasure.

O ardent soul, my friend, the town is dear
Because in every street I feel you near.

SPRING THE CHEAT

The wych-elm shakes its sequins to the ground,
With every wind the chestnut blossoms fall:
Down by the stream the willow-warblers sing,
And in the garden to a merry sound
The moon grass flies. The fantail pigeons call
And sidle on the roof; a murmuring
Of bees about the woodbine-covered wall,
A child's sweet chime of laughter—this is spring.

Luminous evenings when the blackbird sways
Upon the rose and tunes his flageolet,
A sea of bluebells down the woodland ways,—
O exquisite spring, all this—and yet—and yet—
Kinder to me the bleak face of December
Who gives no cheating hopes, but says—"Remember."

THE MAGIC CITY

I HAD not known you skilled in wizardry
Until I trod the pavements at your side,
When sudden at your "Open Sesame"
The magic city flung its portals wide.
Against a sky pale as a chrysolite
I saw, sharp cut in shadow, dome and spire,
Belfry and gabled roof, bewitched by night,
Spangled with flame—my town of heart's desire.

I left it thus at moonrise, and with day
Came back alone—ah! folly! but to find
The glamour fled from street and square and tower.
Vanished my magic city; chill and grey
This drear familiar town, with face unkind
Giving the lie to that enchanted hour.

THE GHOST

My lady, musing at her mirror, said:
"This is my burial night, for I am dead;
Hope dug the grave and laid my sad heart there,
Sorrow was sexton, heavy-footed Care
The lanthorn-bearer, Love in sober stole
Was priest, while fickle Joy stayed but to toll
The bell for me; then Memory graved the stone,
And all being done, they left me there alone.

But though the grave is made, the earth close-
    pressed
About my heart, to-morrow I must rise,
Put on my gay attire, laugh and jest,
Lest one should read the secret in my eyes—
Lest one should know that in this careless host
Of revellers, I linger as a ghost."

THE TRUCE

One made this prayer: "O Christ, I dearly crave
Some little lazy peace to follow death;
A sunny bank where tranquil willows wave
Wind-silvered leaves, and time to draw my breath
Beside a stream knee-deep in arrow-head
And dear forget-me-nots, a gentle spot
Where I may thank my God that I am dead
And all the traffic of the world forgot.

There, dreamless, I shall lie so still—so still,
The cautious moorhen piloting her brood
Will heed me not, the heron stir no quill
For fear of me in that kind solitude.
O grant this truce from pain, this moment's rest,
Before I brace my soul to further test."

ROSA MYSTICA

Our Lady is the mystic rose that bloomed in Nazareth
Against whose blessèd heart there lay the Lord of life and death.

She is the rose without a thorn that grew on Jesse's stem,
The Rose of roses on her breast was lulled in Bethlehem.

To this white rose at God's command the Angel Gabriel came,
With promise of the Blessèd One and message of His Name.

Our Lady is the pale pink rose in whom all fragrance lies,
Her summer was in Jesus' kiss, her sunshine in His eyes.

She is the golden-hearted rose that held our per-
    fect joy;
When in her arms against her heart she clasped
    her heavenly Boy.

Our Lady is the red, red rose upon a royal tree,
Deep red for love and red for grief, the reddest
    rose was she
Whose soul was pierced by sorrow's sword on
    cross-crowned Calvary.

THE WINDS AT BETHLEHEM

When Jesus lay on Mary's knee
   There was no wind nor breeze that stirred,
For Heaven then made minstrelsy
   And all the earth in silence heard.

There was no wind on sea or land,
   No boisterous gale blew loud and wild,
The four great winds came hand in hand
   And stood about the Holy Child.

The four great winds, their pinions furled,
   Came softly in with humble tread;
They saw the Maker of the World
   Upon His lowly manger bed.

The South wind looked with radiant eyes
   Upon this King so small and sweet;
He softly sang Him lullabies
   And knelt adoring at His feet.

THE WINDS AT BETHLEHEM

The West wind like a shepherd clad
   Had brought his pastoral pipes to play;
He piped his music wild and glad
   Until the shadows fled away.

The North wind bowed and knelt him down
   To gaze upon the sight so fair;
He gave the Babe the frosty crown
   That lay upon his tangled hair.

Before that shrine the East wind bent,
   He had strange gifts beyond all price,
Of gold and gems of Orient
   And gums and frankincense and spice.

There was no wind on sea or land,
   But round about the manger bed
The four great winds stood hand in hand
   And worshipped there with wings outspread.

OFFERING

She had no gift to bring her heart's beloved,
So poor she was and sad,
Having no store laid by to cheer the bleak to-
 morrow,
So for his weal she offered all she had—her sorrow.
Who knows but God, compassionate, took heed
Accepting this her treasure,
And on her heart's beloved one in his need
Spent it in fullest measure.

SONIA'S SONG

To hear the angels play their lutes
To hear them sing were good,
But oh! I'd choose to meet my love
Deep in the beechen wood,
With bluebells, bluebells everywhere
About us as we stood.

To see the cherubs play at ball
In every golden street
Were joy enough for Christian souls,
Yet ah! how heaven-sweet
To walk the hills with one I know,
The wild thyme at our feet.

To gaze on all the holy saints,
What should one ask but this?
The sight of them in white array
Might be a sinner's bliss.
But which of them has known the joy
Of my true lover's kiss?

SONIA'S SONG

Have pity on our human hearts,
Dear God, and of Thy grace
Let me be with my own sweet-heart
In some green sunny place.
Oh, let me clasp his hand in mine
And see his happy face.

Then shall I laugh for joy of soul
And merry company
Till all the little seraphs hear
And clap their hands for glee.
Till the blessèd saints and angels laugh
Amid their melody.

THE WISH

O MAN of my heart, I have asked this of God,
A little white house that faces the sun
And yourself to be coming in from the fields
When the day's work is done.

I have told it to God, the wish of my soul,
The little white house at the butt of the hill,
With a handful of land and some grass where the goat
Could be eating her fill.

White walls and nasturtiums, the yellow and red
Climbing upwards to cling to the straw of the thatch,
And a speckledy hen with a dozen fine eggs
That she's wishful to hatch.

THE WISH

The two of us there by the side of the hearth
And the dark lonely night creeping up to the door,
Your smile and your handclasp, oh! man of my heart—
I am asking no more.

HOME

(IN DUBLIN)

I gave her bread and bid her lead me home,
For kilt she was with standing in the cold,
An' she, the creature, not turned eight years old.
She went before me on her small bare feet,
Clutching some papers not yet sold,
Down Westland Row and up Great Brunswick
    Street.
Sometimes she'd turn and peer
Into my face with eyes of fear.
She'd hunch her rags in hope to find some heat,
And stare at shops where they sold things to eat.
Then suddenly she turned,
And where a street lamp burned
Led me along a narrow, dirty lane;
Dim glass and broken pane
Stood for the windows. Every shadowed door
Held children of the poor.
That sheltered from the rain.

HOME

Through one dark door she slipped and bid me come
For this was home.
A narrow stair we had to climb
To reach the topmost floor.
A hundred years of grime
Clung to the walls, and time
Had worked its will. Tenants the like o' these
The landlords don't be planning how they'll please.
A smell was in it made you hold your breath:
These dirty houses pay the tax to death
In babies' lives. But sure they swarm like bees,
Who'd wonder at disease?
The room held little but a depth o' dark;
A woman stirred and spoke the young one's name.
The fire showed no spark,
But presently there came
A slipeen of a girl who made a flame
By burning paper, holding it torch-fashion,
Thinking, maybe, the place would stir compassion.
A dirty mattress and a lidless chest
That served for cradle; near it stood
A table of dark painted wood;
Foreninst the grate a chair

HOME

With three legs good.
The place was bare
Of any sign of food.
The light burnt out. The young one found more
    paper
And kindled it for taper,
This time I saw above the bed
Our Lady in a robe of blue,
A picture of our Saviour's head,
Thorn-crowned. The light fell too
On the child's frightened face,
The wretched dirty place.
And so I spoke of what the priests might do,
Of them that help in such a case.
They'd send the child to some good Home,
And never let her roam
About the streets, half-dead
With cold and hunger.
They'd teach her and befriend her,
Wash her and mend her,
They'd see her clothed and fed,
And in a decent bed.
She'd have her brush and comb.
From every sort of hurt

HOME

They would defend her.
All this I said,
And paused to let them speak.
The child had caught her mother's skirt
And pressed her cheek
Against her arm,
As if she feared some harm.
So, clasping her, the mother shook her head.
"You have a right," said she,
"To leave her here with me.
Heart-broke in such a place she'd be—
The creature loves her home."

THE WIND'S CALL

O Love, the wind would have us for a while,
He called aloud our names about the eaves,
Then passed like smoke across the meadow grass
And with a breath made silver of the leaves.

He cried to us to follow at his heels,
He wound his horn where whitening willows grow.
He stood awhile with ruffled wings to watch
The swayings loosestrife and the river's flow.

Come out, belovèd, let us follow him,
The dripping ivy taps against the pane,
They bid us to the dance in field and wood,
They beckon us—our playmates, wind and rain.

They whisper to us of a hidden place
Within the windswept woods, where boughs bend
    low,
Where two may sit and learn their secret lore,
Where haunted hazels and where rowans grow.

THE WIND'S CALL

The wind is waiting, in your wistful eyes
I see the woods reflected, gay and wild.
What is a world of bricks and men to you?
Come out! Come out! The woods have claimed
    their child.

ELAINE AT ASTOLAT

"And ever she beheld Sir Launcelot wonderfully."—MALORY.

"My heart had contentment," she said,
"Till I saw you pass by,
Bewitching the bird from the bough
And the stars from the sky.
My soul had a sanctuary once
But your shadow fell there,
And the flame of the candles burnt dim
In the chill of the air.
My thoughts had their freedom," she sighed,
"Till you took them in thrall,
Now they follow like birds where you go,
Rising up at your call."

He heeded not, turned not his head
For his heart was his own.
And he passed with a song on his lips
Where she waited alone.

THE PAGE'S SONG OF THE HAPPY LADY

"The princess asked her page to sing, and he, sitting in the twilit window, sang this song to his lute."

There was a lady broke her heart
In two—in two.
She hid the pieces out of sight
And danced and sang the livelong night,
For nothing else remained to do.

"My joy," said she, "was like a bird,
So soon it flew.
And now the winter will be long
With bitter winds and no bird's song . . .
Grey weary days!" As! she spoke true.

She sought no dreary cypress shade,
Nor yew . . . nor yew.
They did not see her eyes were wet,
She gathered pinks and mignonette,
But hidden near her heart was rue.

THE PAGE'S SONG OF THE HAPPY LADY

The Happy Lady she was called,
So few, so few
Can be so careless and so gay,
But if she wept the night away
None knew . . . none knew.

FAËRIES

In the smoke-wraiths blown by a Summer wind,
In the bubbles upon a stream,
In the scent of a rose that was born in June,
In the memory of a dream,
In the joy that sings to a minor key,
In the youth that is young eternally
Lie the silver spell and the golden charm
Of the World of Faërie.

When the sense of a life once lived returns,
When the wind is full of the Spring,
When a freedom nothing can chain awakes
Then I know that the faëries sing;
And they sing a song that would lead us forth,
Ah! it's never to East nor West nor North
But across the evening and through the dusk
To the land of Faërie.

FAËRIES

Their spell has a magic that words would break,
But never the song of a bird
In the splash of a stream that runs through a
    wood
In the soughing trees it is heard.
With a rustle amid the ferny brake,
With the faintest ripple over the lake,
With the sense of a presence near at hand
Come the lords of Faërie.

Men say that the faëries are bravely clad,
But they come not in mortal guise.
No voice has echoed the words they speak
For they talk not in human voice.
In the sudden patter of summer rain,
In a wind that awakes to die again,
In the murmur of birds through summer dawns
Is the speech of Faërie.

TO TIM*

(AN IRISH TERRIER)

O JEWEL of my heart, I sing your praise,
Though you who are alas! of middle age
Have never been to school and cannot read
The weary printed page.

I sing your eyes, two pools in shadowed streams
Where your soul shines in depths of sunny brown,
Alertly raised to read my every mood
Or thoughtfully cast down.

I sing the little nose, so glossy wet,
The well-trained sentry to your eager mind,
So swift to catch the delicate glad scent
Of rabbits on the wind.

Ah! fair to me your wheaten coloured coat,
And fair the darker velvet of your ear,
Ragged and scarred with old hostilities
That never taught you fear.

* Tim died September 8, 1916.

TO TIM

But oh! your heart, where my unworthiness
Is made perfection by love's alchemy,
How often does your doghood's faith cry shame
To my inconstancy.

At last I know the hunter Death will come
And whistle low the call you must obey.
So you will leave me, comrade of my heart,
To take a lonely way.

Some tell me, Tim, we shall not meet again,
But for their loveless logic need we care?
If I should win to Heaven's gate I know
You will be waiting there.

A DOG'S GRAVE

He sleeps where he would wish, in easy call,
Here in a primrose nook beside the wall.
And near the gate, that he may guard us all
Even in death, our faithful seneschal.

I do not think the courteous Cherubim
Will chide him if he waits, nor Seraphim
Summon him hence till we may follow him
Who knew no heav'n without—faithful Tim.

TO SCOTT

(A COLLIE, FOR NINE YEARS OUR FRIEND)

OLD friend, your place is empty now. No more
Shall we obey the imperious deep-mouthed call
That begged the instant freedom of our hall.
We shall not trace your foot-fall on the floor
Nor hear your urgent paws upon the door.
The loud-thumped tail that welcomed one and all,
The volleyed bark that nightly would appal
Our tim'rous errand boys—these things are o'er.

But always yours shall be a household name,
And other dogs must list' your storied fame;
So gallant and so courteous, Scott, you were,
Mighty abroad, at home most debonair.
Now God who made you will not count it blame
That we commend your spirit to His care.

THE MONKEY'S CAROL

KIND Christian souls who pass me by
  On business intent,
I pray you think on such as I
  Who pine in banishment.
    I wear a little coat of red,
    'A little bonnet on my head.
    Kind gentles, throw a coin to me
    And God reward your charity.

My master grinds the music out
  To cheer the sullen street;
The children gather round about
  And dance with joyous feet.
    Have pity on the poor old man
    And give him pennies all who can;
    Have pity on his monkey too,
    And God be pitiful to you.

THE MONKEY'S CAROL

Once long ago my heart was light
  Amongst my brethren in the south,
Fulfilled with joy I slept at night
  The taste of mangoes in my mouth.
     But now I go from door to door.
     Have pity, gentles, on the poor.
     My master is both weak and old,
     And I am trembling in the cold.

Your kitchens have a fragrant scent
  With pies and puddings on each side,
I wish you all much merriment
  And peace and love this Christmastide.
     If you have nuts or fruit for me
     God will reward your charity;
     For if you give the poor their share
     God will not leave your platters bare.

PENSIONERS

My pensioners who daily
Come here to beg their fare,
For all their need dress gaily
And have a jaunty air.
With "Tira—lira—lira—
Now of your charity
Pray help the little brethren
Of noble poverty."

One shines in glossy sable,
One wears a russet coat,
And one who seeks my table
Has red about his throat.
With "Tira—lira—lira—"
Gay waistcoat, speckled vest,
Black cap and fine blue bonnet,
They all come bravely dressed.

PENSIONERS

To them I gladly scatter
In this their time of need,
Heap bread upon their platter
And ask not for my meed,
But in the jocund spring-time
Their songs give back to me
A thousand-fold—my brethren
Of noble poverty.

LOOKERS-ON

My dear, though you and I should never win
Parts in the mumming play of life nor shine
In tarletan, or tinsel, mouthing fine
Sweet sentences beneath a limelight moon—
What odds? The seats are cheap, we'll come within
As lookers-on; watch lover and buffoon
And clap for Columbine and Harlequin.

We'll laugh aloud at hoary Pantaloon,
And know our silly wanton hearts akin
To Punchinello's, fooled by love and wine.
The play and players vanish all too soon,—
To envy them were but a churlish sin;
We will not grudge them flute and violin,
We'll clap for Harlequin and Columbine.

To envy them . . . Ah! yes,—a churlish sin!

FRIENDS

My friends have been like daily bread,
Essential yet unmerited;
As kind as sunshine after rain
And firelight on the window pane:
As kind as harbour lights at sea
Or some familiar melody:
As good as salt my friend to me.

I count them over for love's praise,—
The rascal troop of childhood's days,
The laughter-loving friends of school
Who sighed beneath the selfsame rule.
The lank of limb, the quick of tongue,
With waist-encircling arms we clung,—
So well we loved when we were young.

I found them matched to every mood,
Wise, frivolous or rash or good;
Gay comrades of the winter fire
Oh, answering summertime's desire,
Companions of the sun and wind,
Dear fellow-travellers, proven, kind,
The spirit-kin of heart and mind.

FRIENDS

I bless them all, but ah! most blessed
Be those true friends beyond the rest
Who, silent but yet unafraid,
Have watched and waited, loved and prayed,
When, lone as every soul must be,
The dreary shadows closed on me
In nether-pits of agony.

. . . . . .

With friendship little need I care
For stiffening limbs and whitening hair,
For as the tale of years is told
My friends grow old—they too grow old.
But since death makes worn thing anew
Old bonds shall prove more tried and true,
I'll still love you . . . and you . . . and you.

ANGELIC SERVICE

No angel is so high
But serveth clowns and kings
And doeth lowly things;
He in this serviceable love can see
The symbol of some heavenly mystery,—
So common things grow wings.

No angel bravely dressed
In larkspur-coloured gown,
But he will bend him down
And sweep with careful art the meanest floor,
Singing the while he sweeps and toiling more
Because he wears a crown.

Set water on to boil,
An angel helps thee straight;
Kneeling beside the grate
With pursèd mouth he bloweth up the flame
Chiding the tardy kettle that for shame
Would make an angel wait.

ANGELIC SERVICE

Make thou conserves, the while
Two little cherubs stand
Tip-toe at either hand,
And one would help thee stir, and one would skim
The golden juice that foams about the brim,
So serveth thy command.

And that same toil-worn broom
So humble in thine eyes,
Perchance has donned disguise
And is a seraph on this errand bent,
To show thee service is a sacrament
And Love wears servant's guise.

OUR LADY OF THE LUPINS

Our Lady loves the lily fair
   Who stands so tall and white
With head bowed down in constant prayer
   To Christ, the King of light.

The daisies in the meadow grass
   Right dear she holds them all,
And smiles if she should hap' to pass
   The roses on the wall.

She loves the flowers in their degree
   For each one is a gem
Of worth and beauty fit to be
   In some saint's diadem.

The grave nasturtium on her way
   Lights up its blossom fires
By beauty only can it say
   The love which she inspires.

OUR LADY OF THE LUPINS

Before her feet the blossoms fall
   Because she loves them well,
But on the lupins most of all
   Her eyes delight to dwell.

Each spire is clothed in God's own blue,
   And faith it signifies;
Our Lady's robe is of this hue,
   The colour of the skies.

The lupins' pride of blue and green
   Delights the Mother blessed;
She stands among them as their queen,
   They reach unto her breast.

THE DOCTOR

There's a grassy place they call the Grove, close
    by St. John o' God's,
Where sally willows bloom in spring, gold heads
    on pale-green rods.
The chestnuts brust their swollen buds, a stream
    goes splashing by.
You'll see the young leaves o' the year against a
    rain-washed sky.
And where else would you choose but be there on
    the sun-warmed sods?

'Twas there old Molly often went and rested on
    the grass,
Begging a copper for God's sake of all that she'd
    see pass.
She'd bless them up to Heaven's gate and pledge
    her word to pray
For their salvation if they'd spare a penny for
    some tay.
Their hearts were softer, so she thought, as they
    went home from Mass.

THE DOCTOR

A poor old dirty woman, what way was she at all?
Her skirt all torn to flitters, and rags itself her shawl:
A quare old silly woman, her boots let in the rain,
And sorra stocking to her feet, you'd see her limp with pain,
Letting a sigh at every step an' clutchin' at the wall.

Herself was in it one fine day, when down the path there came
A dacint stranger dressed in black, she couldn't tell his name,
"God save your honour this good day, an' that you'll keep your health;
The saints protect yous," Molly said, "an' send you luck and wealth."
"God save yourself, poor soul," says he, "an' may you have the same."

He stood a minyit watching her, an' she began to whine
The same old tale she always had for thim whose clothes was fine.

She hadn't broken fast that day, an' surely she
    was bet,
A cup o' tay to warm her heart she hadn't tasted
    yet,
An' she so old—just closin' in on seventy-eight or
    nine.

The dacint stranger looked at her, the look of him
    was kind;
Whativer thing it was God knows that brought
    into her mind
The Passionists that came to preach in April was
    a year,
The time the big Retreat was held for all the
    people here,
Fine holy men that scared us well to leave our sins
    behind.

"I know you, Molly, well," says he, "a power of
    times we've met,
Your sight is not so good itself, or maybe you
    forget

THE DOCTOR

The times we've passed, but now you beg and sorra
    coin have I,
But, better still, I know a cure you have a right to
    try,
Take courage now and tell me all, I'll surely cure
    you yet."

She let a laugh to hear him talk, "God help you,
    dear," says she,
" 'Twould take a knowledgeable man to cure the
    likes o' me;
But I've heard of travelling doctors with bottles
    that they sell
At seven an' fi'pence each, no less, that's bound to
    make you well.
I'm thinking, now your honour speaks, it's one of
    thim you'll be."

He let a laugh himself that time: "Ah! Molly,
    there's no saying,
A cure I have for wake and old, and niver talk of
    paying;

Come, tell me of the way you are, the woeful pains
    you feel.
You're stiff to move, and in the church 'tis mortal
    hard to kneel,
And harder still to rise yourself the time you've
    done your praying?"

"Aye, stranger, that's the way I am; they call it
    being old,
And kilt I am with weary roads, with hunger and
    the cold.
But yet, God help me, I was young as any girl
    you'll see,
And had the lads all leppin' up to run and look
    at me,
A fine young figyure of a girl with hair like shiny
    gold."

Old Molly laughed, she rubbed her hands, then
    coughed and held her side,
The poor old withered creature, you'd think she
    would have died

Before she fetched her breath again and found the strength to spake;
"That God may pity me," she gasped, "I'm feeling mortal wake,
The cough it caught a hoult of me to sarve me for my pride.

"There's no lie in it, honey, none! I'm tellin' simple truth,
The lovely girl I was myself when in the flow'r o' youth,
As careless as the month o' May; still, mind yous, tidy-living,
But looks and smiles when girls are young there's little harm in giving."
She smiled, the creature, as she spoke, an' showed one broken tooth.

"The money, stranger, flew those times; I've spent nigh twenty shilling
To buy a pair of laced-up boots, my father he was willing,

An' a lovely feathered hat I wore the times we
    drove to Mass,
The lot of us packed warm and close behind the
    little ass,
But ruinated, faith! it was one day when rain was
    spilling.

"And then I married with himself, and things were
    hard enough,
When he'd drink taken, nothing plazed, and often
    he'd be rough—
That God may pity him, poor soul—we had our
    share of throuble.
The notions in a young girl's mind are like a shiny
    bubble
That will burst the day she marries, for life is
    different stuff.

"The childer came too fast those times, but there
    —God's will is best,
He sends the child, and though you're poor, you've
    got to do the rest.

THE DOCTOR

I never could sit under them, and most had bandy
    legs,
The like of us can't rare a child on butcher's meat
    and eggs;
'Twas lack of nourishment made Pat so wakely in
    his chest.

"He died on us in Loughlinstown, there in a Union
    bed,
And hard it was to bury him, for we were wanting
    bread,
My grief! the next to go was Liz, she died the end
    of May,
I let the sorrow in on me when she had gone
    away.
It seemed my heart was frozen stone, I had no
    tears to shed.

"The Boers they killed poor Terry, that joined
    the Fusiliers;
I saw the other boys come back, and heard the
    people's cheers.

And Mary's in America, but God knows where
    she'll be,
A Christianable daughter would take more heed
    for me;
But not a word she's thought to write this weary
    length o' years.

"My comrade he was taken, too, the drink had him
    destroyed;
He died on me one Christmas time, and wasn't I
    annoyed
To have no bands of crape to wear as token of
    respect,
An' but one coach to follow was the cruel hard
    neglect,
For a dacint funeral was a thing himself would
    have enjoyed.

"Not one of thim is in it now, and here am I
    alone,
With sorra one to welcome me, or place to call my
    own.

The weary world it is to me, for God has sent me sorrow,
I'm badly situated now, with nothing for to-morrow—
An' if I can't pay fi'pence down, my bed may be a stone."

Old Molly lost her breath and coughed as tho' her heart was breakin',
Maybe the stranger pitied her, so thin she was and shakin',
A poor old bag of bones itself inside her ragged shawl.
He caught her hand, she clutched at him, for she was like to fall,
Her heart was thumping at her side, an' all her limbs were achin'.

Through passing clouds the sun shone out and sparkled on the sod
A little shining spear of green was every willow rod,

The stranger looked in Molly's eyes, she struggled for her breath.
She knew his name, poor creature, now—the doctor's name was Death.
"O Christ," she moaned, "receive my soul. Have pity on me, God."

 . . . . . .

Sparrows were chirping, blackbirds sang, their comrades' hearts to please,
And sorra heed they took of her that lay below the trees.
Splash of the stream the silence stirred or beat of pigeon's wing
A squirrel peeped above a bough to see the crumpled thing
Upon the grass, with crusts of bread still lying on her knees.

A robin bolder than the rest hopped down upon her shawl
And picked the bread she couldn't use, then perched upon the wall,

Singing his grace and watching her that was so
    quare an' still,
He thought he had a right, maybe, to go an' take
    his fill;
He lit down on her poor old boot, she never moved
    at all.

A man, was after selling ferns, came through the
    place at last,
His wife that had the basket she couldn't walk so
    fast,
But streeled behind, her ragged skirt flapping at
    either heel;
She chewed, the creature, as she went a bit of
    orange peel,
An' wondered what old heap of rags upon the
    ground was cast.

'Twas Molly that was lying there, and sure himself
    knew well;
He took the pipe out from his mouth, then turned
    and let a yell:

" 'Tis poor old Molly Quin," says he, "d'ye see the
    way she's lying?
An' stiff and cold she is itself, the creature's after
    dying.
Let yous stay here a minyit now, I'll seek for one
    to tell."

The woman put her basket down, and crossed her-
    self and cried:
"May God have mercy on her soul, 'twas all alone
    she died
Like some old crow beside the road, now that's the
    woeful sight.
The pòlis should be warned of this, maybe you
    have a right
To go find one of thim beyant, I'll stay here at her
    side."

He looked at Molly huddled there, the crusts upon
    her knee.
" 'Tis sure enough ourselves will die the self-same
    way," says he:

"Just thravel till we drop down dead and lie in any
  ditch—
A dacint death and burying are meant for thim
  that's rich.
Let you stay here now till I bring the pòlis back
  with me."

Close by the wall there runs a path through tangle
  of great weeds,
And one cuts straight across the grass and to the
  village leads.
The woman watched her comrade go, then stared
  up at the sky
For fear would Molly peep at her from out a half-
  closed eye.
She fumbled in her ragged skirt until she found
  her beads,

Then started muttering aloud, her lips moved fast
  in prayer.
A little wind that stirred the grass went ruffling
  through her hair;

It blew the rags of Molly's shawl against her pale,
    dead face,
And all the while it told the birds that Spring was
    in the place.
What heed, the creatures, did they take that death
    itself was there?

The woman prayed, but watched a wren upon an
    ivy wreath,
A nest was hidden somewhere safe in the old wall
    beneath.
The comrade bird upon a branch his small sweet
    song was singing,
Then on a sudden from St. John's the Angelus was
    ringing:
A passing bell it was for one cured by the doctor,
    Death.

SAILS

Where Taw flows out from Barwin Town,
Where Taw flows out to sea,
The bonny boats sail up and down
Upon the Estuary;
They carry—Heaven knows what store—
Past Instow and past Appledore,
With sunburnt jolly men aboard
From Westward Ho and Bideford.

Where Taw flows out from Barwin Town,
The full tide brings the sails
Of orange hue or tawny brown
That weather many gales;
And some are white as wind-blown foam
And others red as Devon loam,
With goodly bales they come and go
To Bideford and Westward Ho.

SAILS

Where Taw flows out from Barwin Town
I dearly long to be,
With sails of tangerine and brown
To sail with you to sea.
Who'd care at all if we were poor
At Instow or at Appledore.
We'd sail—so be we could afford—
To Westward Ho and Bideford.

THE REBEL

O GOD, when I kneel down to pray
Heed only then the words I say
And do not listen to my heart
Which mutters to itself apart.
I say, "God bless my enemies."
Then take my word and bless them, please;
Be deaf to that fierce self which still
Murmurs, "But ah! I wish them ill!"

I say, "Dear God, Thy will is best,"
But loud and angry in my breast
This untamed heart is crying, "Nay,
"Not Thine, but mine; I want my way."
Two selves that struggle—one loves sin,
And one loves God. Say, which shall win?
Be deaf, Lord, to the evil voice
And give my rebel heart no choice.

AEROPLANES AND DRAGONFLIES

A SHIMMER, a glimmer beside the stream;
Blue flame, green flame, jewels of a dream;
Emeralds that quiver above the water weeds;
Sapphires that shiver among the spear-like reeds.
Gems that have wings, that chase and float and
    rise;
Gems of June's casket—dragonflies.

Over sky-fields, down streams of windy space
Hover great aeroplanes that swoop and chase.
Surely the war gods shout to hear them hum—
"Brother! Young gods with thunderbolts are
    come.
Greater than us, yet wearing man's disguise,
Sons of Thor's breed who ride on dragonflies."

THE TRYST

"Until we meet again"—ah, happy meeting!
But, weary with the town, I crave God's pity
And ask cool meadows for that promised greeting,
Far from the jewelled gates, the shining city;

Wide meadows where the buttercups are golden,
No jewels there but eyebright and red clover,
A stream that creeps by willows grey and olden,
Waters with weeds and flowers 'broidered over.

Great dragon flies that flit and gleam and quiver,
Bees that make silence music by their humming;
—So still a place I'd ask of God the giver,
Where I might wait the moment of your coming;

Far from the thronging saints, the seraph choir
I'd see the dawning of my heart's desire.

THE END

www.ingramcontent.com/pod-product-compliance
Ingram Content Group UK Ltd.
Pitfield, Milton Keynes, MK11 3LW, UK
UKHW032254010225
454531UK00005B/92